First World War
and Army of Occupation
War Diary
France, Belgium and Germany

19 DIVISION
Divisional Troops
C Squadron 1/1 Yorkshire Dragoons
26 June 1915 - 9 May 1916

WO95/2067/1

The Naval & Military Press Ltd
www.nmarchive.com
Published in association with The National Archives

Published by

The Naval & Military Press Ltd

Unit 10 Ridgewood Industrial Park,

Uckfield, East Sussex,

TN22 5QE England

Tel: +44 (0) 1825 749494

www.naval-military-press.com

www.nmarchive.com

This diary has been reprinted in facsimile from the original. Any imperfections are inevitably reproduced and the quality may fall short of modern type and cartographic standards.

© **Crown Copyright**
Images reproduced by permission of The National Archives, London, England, 2015.

Contents

Document type	Place/Title	Date From	Date To
Heading	19 Div-'C' Sqn 1/1 Yorkshire Dragoons Jun 1915-May 1916		
Heading	19th Division 'C' Sqdn 1-1st Yorkshire Dragoons. Jun 1915-May 1916		
Heading	19th Division "C" Squadron Yorks: Dragoons. Vol I June to Oct 15		
Heading	War Diary of "C" Squadron 1/1st Yorkshire Dragoons from June 26th 1915-to October 31st 1915 Volume I		
War Diary	Bulford	26/06/1915	19/07/1915
War Diary	Havre	20/07/1915	23/07/1915
War Diary	Hazebrouck	24/07/1915	24/07/1915
War Diary	Manqueville	29/07/1915	31/07/1915
War Diary	Beaupre	03/08/1915	05/08/1915
War Diary	Le Vert Bois	13/08/1915	30/08/1915
War Diary	Quentin	01/09/1915	25/09/1915
War Diary	Locon	25/09/1915	03/10/1915
War Diary	Quentin	06/10/1915	31/10/1915
Heading	19th Division "C" Sq. Yorkshire Dragoons. Nov 15 Vol 2		
Heading	War Diary of 19th Div. Cavalry Sqdn. from November 1st to November 30th Volume 1		
War Diary	La Pannerie	01/11/1915	22/11/1915
War Diary	La Haye	23/11/1915	30/11/1915
Heading	19th Div "C" Sq: Yorkshire Dragoons: Vol: 3		
Heading	War Diary of "C" Squadron-1/1st Yorkshire Dgns. 19th Division from December 1st to December 31st 1915. (Volume 3)		
War Diary	La Haye	01/12/1915	05/12/1915
War Diary	Paradis	07/12/1915	31/12/1915
Heading	C Sq. Yorks. Vol: 4 Jan 16		
Heading	War Diary of "C" Squadron-1/1st Yorkshire Dgns. from January 1st to January 31st 1916 (Volume VII)		
War Diary	Paradis	01/01/1916	25/01/1916
War Diary	La Haye	26/01/1916	31/01/1916
Heading	War Diary of "C" Sqdn. 1/1st Yorkshire Dragoons. from February 1st to February 29th 1916 (Volume 5)		
War Diary	La Haye	01/02/1916	17/02/1916
War Diary	La Gorgue	19/02/1916	29/02/1916
Heading	War Diary of "C" Squadron-1/1 Yorkshire Dragoons from March 1st to March 31st 1916 Volume IX		
War Diary	La Gorgue	01/03/1916	31/03/1916
Heading	War Diary Of "C" Sqdn. 1/1st Yorkshire Dragoons From April 1st To April 30th 1916 (Volume 9)		
War Diary		02/04/1916	17/04/1916
War Diary	La Haye	17/04/1916	19/04/1916
War Diary	St. Quentin	20/04/1916	21/04/1916
War Diary	Fressin	22/04/1916	30/04/1916
Heading	War Diary of "C" Squadron, 1/1st Q. O. Yorkshire Dragoons From 1st to 9th May 1916 (Volume)		
War Diary	Fressin	01/05/1916	09/05/1916

WO95/2067

19 Div – 'C' Sqn

1/1 Yorkshire Dragoons

Jan 1915 – May 1916

19TH DIVISION

'C' SQDN 1-1ST YORKSHIRE DRAGOONS.

JUN 1915 - MAY 1916.

To 2nd CORPS

19th Hussars

121/7593

"C" Squadron Yorks: Dgns.
Vol I
June to Oct 15

May '16

Confidential
War Diary

of

"C" Squadron 1/1st Yorkshire Dragoons
from June 26th 1915 to October 31st 1915

Volume I

Army Form C. 2118.

I 80

WAR DIARY
or
INTELLIGENCE SUMMARY.
(Erase heading not required.)

Instructions regarding War Diaries and Intelligence Summaries are contained in F. S. Regs., Part II. and the Staff Manual respectively. Title pages will be prepared in manuscript.

Place	Date	Hour	Summary of Events and Information	Remarks and references to Appendices
	1915			
BULFORD	June 26		'C' Squadron - 1/1st Q.O. Yorkshire Dragoons arrived at BULFORD from SCARBORO' to act as Divisional Cavalry to the 19th Division, as per War Office Orders.	
			The Squadron encamped in BULFORD FIELDS and remained here till July 19th equiping and preparing for service abroad.	
	July 19	12 noon	One half Squadron under MAJOR J. L. INGHAM entrained for SOUTHAMPTON and embarked on the "HUANCHACO" for HAVRE.	
		1.30 pm	The remaining half Squadron under CAPTN. R. THOMPSON entrained for SOUTHAMPTON and embarked on the "KYEBASSA" for HAVRE. Established Officers 135 N.C.O's men 1 2 R.A.M.C. Strength on embarkation 6 Officers 134 N.C.O's men 1 R.A.M.C.	
HAVRE	July 20	5.0 am	Both boats arrived at HAVRE after smooth crossing, and disembarked and marched to rest camp in HAVRE.	
	21	10. am	Entrained with Squadron and Veterinary Mobile Corps for ST. OMER.	
	22	5 am	Arrived ST. OMER; detrained marched to SERQUES. Arrived here 10.30 am + billeted for the night	
	23	7 am	Marched from SERQUES to HAZEBROUCK arrived at 2.0 pm mid-day halt of	

Army Form C. 2118.

II 91

WAR DIARY
or
INTELLIGENCE SUMMARY.
(Erase heading not required.)

Instructions regarding War Diaries and Intelligence Summaries are contained in F. S. Regs., Part II. and the Staff Manual respectively. Title pages will be prepared in manuscript.

Place	Date	Hour	Summary of Events and Information	Remarks and references to Appendices
	10/5		2 hours hunter near WALLON CAPPEL.	
HAZEBROUCK	July 24	7.30am	Marched to MANQUEVILLE, arrived 12. 0 noon	
MANQUEVILLE	29		Remained here til 30st.	
	30		Marched to BEAUPRÉ. Bivvid in field.	
	31		Present strength of Squadron 6 Officers 133 N.C.O's men + R.A.M.C	
BEAUPRÉ	Aug 3		Marched to REGNIER LE CLERC Bivied in field.	
	5		Marched to LE VERT BOIS.	
LE VERT BOIS	13		Was ordered to find a guard of 1 Cpl + 3 men over Rivers trenches recently made. Two positions in all.	
			Range cards were made for these positions.	
	26		Received orders to furnish guard of 1 Cpl + 2 men to relieve 57th Bde. at pot. CEMETERY RIGHT.	
			Received Operation Order No. 6. 19th Divn (Orders to take up a new line from GRENADIER ROAD to FARM CORNER) Also received March Table.	
	30	10 am	Marched to QUENTIN as per march table + bivied here.	
			Present strength of Squadron 6 Officers 134 men + 1 R.A.M.C	

Army Form C. 2118.

WAR DIARY
or
INTELLIGENCE SUMMARY.
(Erase heading not required.)

Instructions regarding War Diaries and Intelligence Summaries are contained in F. S. Regs., Part II. and the Staff Manual respectively. Title pages will be prepared in manuscript.

Place	Date	Hour	Summary of Events and Information	Remarks and references to Appendices
QUENTIN	1915 Sept. 1		Received orders that Divisional Cavalry were to undertake drainage operations in forward area.	
	2		Made second reconnaissance of 'A' drain with MAJOR ELLIOTT A.R.E. G.	
	3		Made personal reconnaissance with MAJOR ELLIOTT of LOISNE Riv. and N. part of 'B' drain as far as British lines	
			Commenced work on 'A' drain at ESTAMINET CORNER.	
	11		Stopped working on 'A' drain by div. owing to laying of cable.	
	13		Commenced working on communication trenches at LE PLANTIN.	
	15		Commenced working on 'B' drain under Reserve trenches.	
	18		Wired to take part in a Scheme with mobile machine gun section. marched to LILLERS arriving at 10.0 a.m.	
	22		Received Divisional orders No. 9. Coy No 74.	
	25	9.15 am	Marched to hills near LOCON. Immediate Divisional Headquarters Guard.	
LOCON			Received instructions re "Clearing of Battlefield". Medical arrangements made for the evacuation of wounded at 2 advanced stations. Two main dressing stations also established. The following general arrangements were made - The Divnl. Squadron, Divnl. Cyclists assisted by the Divisional Corps to perform	

T2134. W.W708-776. 500000. 4/15. Sr.J.C.&S.

Army Form C. 2118.

WAR DIARY
or
INTELLIGENCE SUMMARY.
(Erase heading not required.)

Instructions regarding War Diaries and Intelligence Summaries are contained in F.S. Regs., Part II. and the Staff Manual respectively. Title pages will be prepared in manuscript.

Place	Date	Hour	Summary of Events and Information	Remarks and references to Appendices
			All duties in connection with :- I- Burial of Prisoners II- Burial of Dead III- Collection & disposal of War Material, until they are required for duty as Mounted Troops for the Advance.	
	Sept 28		Received Divisional Orders No. 10.	
	30		Received Order to march to new area.	
			Received Operation Orders No. 11.	
	Oct 3		Passed Strength of Squadron - 6 Officers, 132 N.C.O's & men & 1 R.A.M.C.	
			Marched to Billets at QUENTIN.	
QUENTIN	6		Received instructions & defence scheme for Divisional Area. Received Divisional Orders No. 12.	
			Commenced work on clearing waterway in rear of British lines near PIONEER and LOTHIAN ROADS. Weather = for five = ditch dry.	
	11			
	18		Received Operation Orders No. 13.	
	19		Received Operation Orders No. 14.	
			Received orders to march to new billets.	
	20		Marched to new Billets near LA BASSEE CANAL.	

Army Form C. 2118.

84

WAR DIARY
or
INTELLIGENCE SUMMARY.
(Erase heading not required.)

Place	Date	Hour	Summary of Events and Information	Remarks and references to Appendices
	1915 Oct 27		Commenced work on clearing waterway near SHETLAND ROAD. Weather becoming very wet.	
	31		Commenced building stables for Horses. Recvd Strength of Squadron - 6 Officers (including 1 attached to D.H.Q.) 127 N.C.O's. men & R.A.M.C.	

J F Shearn
Major
O.C. 19th Div. Squadron
Inns Dragoons

19th Kurosawa

"C" Sp: Yakshui Bro.
vol 2

121/7693

Nov 15

Confidential
War Diary

of

19th Div. Cavalry Sqdn.

From November 1st to November 30th

Volume 1

Army Form C. 2118.

VI

WAR DIARY
or
INTELLIGENCE SUMMARY.
(Erase heading not required.)

Instructions regarding War Diaries and Intelligence Summaries are contained in F.S. Regs., Part II. and the Staff Manual respectively. Title pages will be prepared in manuscript.

Place	Date	Hour	Summary of Events and Information	Remarks and references to Appendices
LA PANNERIE	1915 Nov 1		Scheme for defence of Divisional Area received. Tracks made of parts affording Divisional Boundary.	
	2 + 3		Weather - Very heavy rain. Work on "A" drain becoming increasingly difficult owing to depth of water.	
	4 6 8		Engaged on "A" drain.	
	9		Heavy rains prevented work on "A" drain.	
			Recommenced work on above drain. A party of men returning from the RUE DE BOIS. One sergeant was wounded. This was the only casualty.	
	10		Commenced work on the part of "A" drain near ARGYLLE ROAD. Recent heavy rains have been exceedingly difficult. Communication reached 3'0" deep in many parts.	
	11.12.13		Provided 1 Corporal + 5 men for Road Patrol. Continued work near ARGYLLE ROAD.	
	12		Furnished 1 Corporal 14 men as escort to G.O.C. XI Corps.	
	15		Discontinued work near ARGYLLE ROAD.	

Army Form C. 2118.

VII
87

WAR DIARY
or
INTELLIGENCE SUMMARY.
(Erase heading not required.)

Instructions regarding War Diaries and Intelligence Summaries are contained in F.S. Regs., Part II. and the Staff Manual respectively. Title pages will be prepared in manuscript.

Place	Date	Hour	Summary of Events and Information	Remarks and references to Appendices
	Nov 16/6/21		Evening cleaning horse Picketry.	
	22		Received instructions to march into Reserve area (Operation Orders No 18)	
LA HAYE	23	8:30am	Marched to new billets at LA HAYE. Commenced building stables for horses.	
	24		Received Programme of Proposed Training while in Reserve.	
	25	6:30	Engaged in building shelters. Present Strength of Squadron = 6 Officers (including 1 attached to S.H.Q.) 120 N.C.O.s & men + 1 R.A.M.C.	

J.H. Hain
Major

C. SQDN. 1/1st Q.O.Y.D.

"C. M: Yakshini Opus.
Vol: 3

12/7936

Confidential

War Diary

of

"E" Squadron - 1st Yorkshire Dgns.
19th Division

From December 1st to December 31st 1915.
(Volume 6.) 3

Army Form C. 2118.

87/3

VIII

WAR DIARY
or
INTELLIGENCE SUMMARY.
(Erase heading not required.)

Instructions regarding War Diaries and Intelligence Summaries are contained in F. S. Regs., Part II. and the Staff Manual respectively. Title pages will be prepared in manuscript.

Place	Date	Hour	Summary of Events and Information	Remarks and references to Appendices
LA HAYE	1915 Dec.1-3		Engaged on building horse shelters.	
	4		Received instructions to march into new Billets.	
	5	9.0 a.m.	Marched into new Billets at PARADIS. Owing to continual wet weather, the Roads	
			near QUENTIN and PARADIS are, in many places, under water.	
PARADIS	7		Measures taken to clean Dykes, ditches &c.	
	10		Party given hand to clear out Dyke at QUENTIN, but found this was being done by Labour Corps. Roads now in much better condition.	
	11-12		Exercising horses, improving billets, Horse Shelter lines, drainage &c.	
	13		Provided a Fatigue Party of 1 Cpl. 170 men for the R.E.	
	15		Provided a Corporal + 4 men as despatch riders for the Signal Co.	
	17.20		Recommenced cleaning out Dykes. Weather very wet.	
	20		Received draft of 5 men of the 3/1 2 Yorkshire Dragoons from the Base.	
	20-24		Exercising horses, improving billets horse lines &c.	
	25		Arrangements made for Xmas dinners for the troops.	
	26		Horses & Mules inoculated with "MALLEIN" by the Vety. Officer.	
	28		The inoculation was very satisfactory, no re-action taking place.	

T2134. Wt. W708-776. 500000. 4/15. Sir J. C. & S.

Army Form C. 2118.

87C

WAR DIARY
or
INTELLIGENCE SUMMARY.
(Erase heading not required.)

Place	Date	Hour	Summary of Events and Information	Remarks and references to Appendices
	28-31		Lewis guns overhauled, and new Lewis gun bi-weekly practice for all ranks, with new Luke Kernels instituted. N.C.O.'s instruction practice. Strength of Squadron 123 N.C.O.'s + men, 1 R.A.M.C. The weather this month has been very mild. Much rain + wind.	XI

R Ryan Major
O.C. 13th DIV. CAVALRY SQDN.

"C"śś: Yalki: Strc:
tot: 4
Tan 'w

Confidential War Diary of "C" Squadron – 1/1st Yorkshire Dgns.
from January 1st to January 31st 1916
(Volume VII.)

Army Form C. 2118.

WAR DIARY
or
INTELLIGENCE SUMMARY.
(Erase heading not required.)

Instructions regarding War Diaries and Intelligence Summaries are contained in F.S. Regs., Part II. and the Staff Manual respectively. Title pages will be prepared in manuscript.

89

Place	Date	Hour	Summary of Events and Information	Remarks and references to Appendices
PARADIS	1916 June 1		Received instructions to furnish from this date, 1 Cpl. & 4 men as Despatch Riders with Signal Co. at D.H.Q.	
	1		Capt. P. Thompson invalided home to England with Jaundice.	
	3		Squadron inspected by G.O.C. 19th Divn.	
	12		Scheme - Patrolling &c.	
	13-18		Improvements made to Billets & Horse Standings.	
	17		Major F.W. Leighton returned to England on a month's Munition Course. Lieut C.J. Hirst (temporary in command of Squadron.	
	19 & 20		Acting on instructions from D.H.Q. survey made of state of all wire East of, & including the CROIX BARBEE system.	
	21		Plan of above prepared & submitted to D.H.Q.	
	"		Received Div. Orders to "training whilst in Army Reserve."	
	21 & 22		Furnished large fatigue parties for D.H.Q. (Camp Commandant).	
	23		Received draft of 6 men from Base.	
	"		Received Orders to proceed to Reserve Area.	
	25		Moved into Billets at LA HAYE, vacated by Royal Wilts. Germany.	

Army Form C. 2118.

90

WAR DIARY
or
INTELLIGENCE SUMMARY.

XI

(Erase heading not required.)

Place	Date	Hour	Summary of Events and Information	Remarks and references to Appendices
LA HAYE	26-30		Improving Horse Shelters &c	
	29		In conformance with instructions, commenced training as per programme submitted to S.A.9.	
	30		Received draft of 2 men from Base	
	31		Strength of Squadron — 4 Officers (detached to S.H.Q.) 128 N.C.O's men & Rank. Weather — very mild.	

B. Elliot Lieut
for O.C. "D" Sqn
31.10.19

"9"

Confidential

War Diary

of

"C" Sqdn. 1/1st Yorkshire Dragoons.

from February 1st to February 29th 1916

(Volume 5.)

Army Form C. 2118.

92

WAR DIARY
or
INTELLIGENCE SUMMARY.
(Erase heading not required.)

XII

Instructions regarding War Diaries and Intelligence Summaries are contained in F. S. Regs., Part II. and the Staff Manual respectively. Title pages will be prepared in manuscript.

Place	Date	Hour	Summary of Events and Information	Remarks and references to Appendices
	1916			
LA HAYE	Feby 1		In compliance with instructions provided, until further Orders, 1 N.C.O & 3 men to patrol Roads at LE SART in vicinity of Rifle Range.	
	" 3		Inspection of Practice in Smoke Helmets.	
	" 5		According to instructions from D.H.Q furnished 1 Officer + 8 men as signallers to take part in scheme.	
	1-15		Carried out programme of training as submitted weekly to D.H.Q	
	16		Received instructions to proceed to fresh Billets.	
	17	8.30 a.m.	Marched to fresh Billets near LA GORGUE vacated by Household Cavalry Divisional Sqdn.	
LA GORGUE	19-20		Cleaning up Billets + Horse Lines.	
	20		Received instructions to terminate provision of Rifle Range Patrol.	
	23-25		Provided party to assist A.P.M. in searching buildings in Divn. Area for Government Stores &c.	
	25-29		Acting on instructions from D.H.Q surveyed wire in Divn. Area.	
	" 29		Received draft of 2 Officers from 3rd Line.	
			Strength of Sqdn. 120 N.C.Os men, 1 R.A.M.C. - Weaker - killed first arms steel later.	

Yorks Drag
Vol 6
/93
4

Confidential

War Diary

of

"C" Squadron ~ 1/1 Yorkshire Dragoons

from March 1st to March 31st 1916.

Volume IX

Army Form C. 2118.

94

XIII

WAR DIARY
or
INTELLIGENCE SUMMARY.
(Erase heading not required.)

Place	Date	Hour	Summary of Events and Information	Remarks and references to Appendices
LA GORGUE	1916 March 1-20		According to instructions received from C.R.E. provided working parties each day to load wagons & convoy same to forward area & unload.	
	2		Completed description & map of survey of wire in Div. Area & submitted same to D.H.Q.	
	5		Received draft of 6 men from 3/1st Yorkshire Dragoons. The Colonel of the Regiment raised the Squadron.	
	8-11		Muster parade for inspection of Smoke Helmets.	
	10		Received draft of 8 men from 3/1st Yorkshire Dragoons.	
	14		Provided 2 Orderlies for 58th Inf. Bde. till further notice.	
	20			
	21-31		According to instructions received from D.H.Q. provided working parties to build breastworks at PONT LOGY. One man received slight bullet wound in wrist. During the month improvements were done to the Billets, including the building of wash houses. Strength of Squadron 122 N.C.Os & men & 2 R.A.M.C. Weather – Changeable at first, including snow. Fine & warm later.	

CONFIDENTIAL

WAR DIARY
OF
"C" SQDN. 1ST YORKSHIRE DRAGOONS

FROM APRIL 1ST TO APRIL 30TH 1916.

(VOLUME 9)

Army Form C. 2118.

96

WAR DIARY
or
INTELLIGENCE SUMMARY.
(Erase heading not required.)

XIV

Instructions regarding War Diaries and Intelligence Summaries are contained in F. S. Regs., Part II. and the Staff Manual respectively. Title pages will be prepared in manuscript.

Place	Date	Hour	Summary of Events and Information	Remarks and references to Appendices
	1916			
	Ap. 2		Acting under instructions from G.S. 19th Divn. carried out Field Training each Coy.	
	3		Received Copy of 19th Divn Defence Scheme.	
	3-7		Provided working parties to erect Defence works at PONT LOGY.	
	3-5		Provided working parties for 19th D.A.C.	
	5		Received Copy of 19th Divn Order No. 38.	
	.		1 Officer & 4 Sgt. commenced Course of Instruction at 19th Divn. School at MERVILLE	
	8		Capt R. Thomson assumed command of Coy. & 19th Divn. Mounted Troops with the temporary rank of Major, during the absence in England of Major J. L. Ingham.	
	10		2 N.C.O's commenced Course of Instruction in Hotchkiss Guns at CAMIERS.	
	11		Paraded 1 Officer & 30 men to represent Divn. Cavalry at Presentation of Decorations by G.O.C. 1st Army.	
	11-14		Provided working parties to erect wire defences at CROIX BARBEE.	
	12		Received Copy of 19th Divn. Order No. 39.	
	13		Provided working party for XI Corps. MERVILLE.	
	15-16		Provided party for Traffic Control duties under A.P.M.	
	17	9.30	According to instructions received from H.Q. 19th Divn., Sqdn. marched and Rec. Billets at	

Army Form C. 2118.

96D

XV

WAR DIARY
or
INTELLIGENCE SUMMARY.
(Erase heading not required.)

Instructions regarding War Diaries and Intelligence Summaries are contained in F.S. Regs., Part II. and the Staff Manual respectively. Title pages will be prepared in manuscript.

Place	Date	Hour	Summary of Events and Information	Remarks and references to Appendices
LA HAYE	17		LA HAYE.	
			Received Copy of 19th Divn Order No. 40.	
			Received draft of 10 men from 3/1st Yorkshire Dragoons.	
			Men provided for escort to G.O.C. XI Corps, returned to Sclm. Also N.C.O.'s issued with Signal Co. 19th Divn.	
	19	7.30 am	Sqdn. left LA HAYE & marched to ST. QUENTIN (AIRE)	
ST. QUENTIN	20		G.O.C. 19th Divn inspected Sqdn.	
	21	9.0 am	Sqdn. left ST. QUENTIN and marched to FRESSIN to undergo Course of training in work of Divn. Mounted Troops & temporarily attached to 3rd Cavalry Division.	
FRESSIN	22		G.O.C. 3rd Cavalry Divn inspected horses, and addressed Officers N.C.O.'s of 19th Divn Mounted Troops (Cavalry + Cyclists)	
	23		Received Syllabus of training.	
	23-30		Carried out training.	
	25		3 N.C.O.'s commenced 1 weeks training in Hotchkiss Guns at 2nd Cav. Div. School.	
			Received draft of 5 men from 2/1st Yorkshire Dragoons.	
	30		Strength of Sqdn. 12.8 N.C.O.'s issued, 1 Intptr., 2 R.A.U.C, 1 A.V.G M.I attached	

Army Form C. 2118.

97

XVI

WAR DIARY
or
INTELLIGENCE SUMMARY.
(Erase heading not required.)

Place	Date	Hour	Summary of Events and Information	Remarks and references to Appendices
			From Reg. Head Qrs. Weather - Changeable at first. Very fine & warm later.	

R Kentjener Capt
C/ Ayder 1/1st Ydh Sqn

C. Squad
Yorks Dragoons
Vol. 8

98 19

Confidential

War Diary
— of —

"C" Squadron, 1/1st Q.O. Yorkshire Dragoons

From 1st to 9th May 1916.

(Volume   )

Army Form C. 2118.

WAR DIARY
or
INTELLIGENCE SUMMARY.
(Erase heading not required.)

XVII

Place	Date	Hour	Summary of Events and Information	Remarks and references to Appendices
FRESSIN	1916 May 1 to 5th		Carried out training as per Syllabus.	
	6		Received instructions to proceed to YSEUX to-morrow. Above instructions cancelled.	
		9	According to instructions the Squadron proceeded to HAZEBROUCK where the Regiment was assembling to act as Cavalry to II Corps under re-distribution Scheme.	

W Thompson Rogers O.C. "C" Squadron 11th Q.O. Yorkshire Dragoons

www.ingramcontent.com/pod-product-compliance
Lightning Source LLC
Chambersburg PA
CBHW081502160426
43193CB00014B/2569